A Maggie & Rose Activity Book

This Book is Totally Rubbish

meet Maggie, Rose, Oscar and Bentley.
They are having a "totally rubbish day" where they will
reuse oodles of things and invent new stuff to play with.
They're doing this to help the environment
and to become eco superheroes.

ECO is short for "ecology", which is a big word that means all the living things in the world … ever.
OODLES is a funny word meaning "lots", which rhymes with "noodles".

WALKER BOOKS
AND SUBSIDIARIES
LONDON · BOSTON · SYDNEY · AUCKLAND

Super Top-Secret Club Room

This room is so amazingly secret that only three people and a dog know about it in the entire world. And now you.

Using the computer, Maggie found out that...
REDUCE means to make stuff from things at home instead of buying new stuff.
REUSE means using stuff again ... and again ... and again.
RECYCLE means to make something out of something else.
It's important to know these words – they're going to be used a lot.

All activites in this book should be done with help from a grown-up.

M & R

Eco Superhero Outfits

Every eco superhero needs a proper eco superhero outfit! Maggie has discovered a great way to make outfits for all her friends.

The Mask

First you'll need a mask, which will absolutely stop people knowing who you really are!

1. Draw a mask shape onto a triple layer of newspaper. Make sure the eye holes are big enough and far enough apart for you to see out of. Cut out the three layers of mask.

2. Carefully tape the edges together with sticky tape.

3. Use a pencil to poke a hole in each side of the mask.

4. Cut two lengths of string, each long enough to wind around your head. Thread each one through a pencil hole and tie a knot around the outside of the mask to secure it.

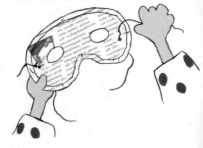

Now, tie the mask onto your head!

Wow! Who are you?

The Cape

Second you'll need a cape, because all eco superheroes wear capes. It's a rule. They just do!

1. Take two large pieces of newspaper and tape the edges together. This will make your cape stronger.

2. Take the top two corners and scrunch them up as shown. Wind some string or sticky tape around each corner to make sure it stays scrunched up.

Remember: eco superhero capes cannot make you fly. Only aeroplanes and helicopters can do that and they don't wear capes, do they?

3. Measure out two lengths of string. Each one should be long enough to wrap around the top of your arm twice. Make arm holes by tying the two pieces of string to the two scrunched up corners.

4. Paint a recycling sign on your cape.

Eco Train

Oscar's mummy has just had a delivery and it came in lots of boxes. This has given Oscar and Bentley an idea — they are going to make a train to collect recycling in. Oscar likes trains because they are fast. Bentley likes trains because they remind him of a string of sausages.

STUFF TO USE

4 cardboard boxes

Sticky tape

Old magazines

16 paper plates

Bottle tops

Tin foil

Glue

String

1. To make the driver's cab, fold in the top and bottom of one box and sticky tape them down.

2. Decorate the cab by gluing pages from old magazines to the outside, like wallpaper.

Glass

3. Make four wheels for your cab using paper plates decorated with old bottle tops and bits of tin foil. Stick your wheels onto the cab with glue.

4. Now make some carriages for your train. Make them in the same way as you made the driver's cab, but this time only fold in the top of the box and leave the bottom so they will hold your recycling. That's the really clever bit. Decorate your carriages and add wheels.

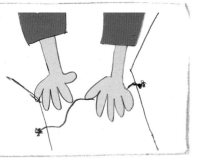

5. Write on the side of each carriage what it will hold: paper, glass, plastic.

Glass

6. Join the carriages together by firmly attaching string with sticky tape. Make sure your driver's cab is at the front.

Now you're ready to go.
CHOO-CHOO!

Paper

Plastic

Recycling Stomp

It's very important to recycle boxes — and playing this game makes it much more fun. Oscar likes to pick songs with loud drumming to stomp to.

STUFF TO USE

Recycling bag

Lots of boxes

Music

1. First fill a bag with boxes that haven't been flattened. How many can you get in?

2. Practise your stomp. You need to jump as high as you can and land on two feet. To make it harder, try hopping on one foot. Before you stomp on a box, always check there's nothing in it, like an egg. Or Bentley.

3. Now get all the boxes you have and pile them up as high as you can. Turn on your favourite song and do the recycling stomp.

4. When the boxes are as flat as can be, see how many you can fit in the bag. It'll be oodles more than you could at the start!

Super Paper-Mâché

Paper is really useful stuff, but we usually have to chop down trees to make it. Trees help the earth to breathe, so chopping them down is bad. Luckily, Maggie has found a good way to reuse newspaper and make fun things to play with – genius!

1. This will get messy, so cover the area where you are going to work in lots of newspaper.

2. Tear some more newspaper into different sized strips – long strips for bigger areas, small squares for smaller areas.

3. Mix together flour and water to make glue (see the Eco Art Supplies page). Dip your paper strips in the glue and apply to the surface you want to cover.

4. Repeat until your object is covered in multiple layers of gluey paper. Leave to dry.

Paper-Mâché Inspiration Page

Maggie has made some plates to have a tea party with her teddies.

1. Find some old plates.
2. Paper-mâché the top surface of each plate.
3. Trim the edges and leave to dry.
4. Peel off the real plate.
5. Paint with PVA glue or egg whites to finish.

Rose has made some pretty goblets for Maggie's tea party.

1. Find some old plastic cups.
2. Turn upside down and paper-mâché around the outside.
3. Find some fun things to decorate with. Beads and feathers are great. Stick these on.
4. Leave to dry.

Oscar has made a helmet so he can be a knight.

1. Blow up a balloon to around the size of your head and tie tightly.
2. Wedge it in a shoe box to keep it steady.
3. Paper-mâché the top half of the balloon and leave to dry.
4. Remove from balloon. Check it fits your head and then attach string to fasten it.
5. Paint it whatever colour you like!

Eco Pass the Parcel

Have some fun with Dad's newspaper (after he's read it) — play pass the parcel Maggie and Rose style.

STUFF TO USE

Small pieces of coloured paper

Felt-tip pens

Newspaper

Sticky tape

A prize

Music

Lots of friends

1. Make up eight to twelve silly things to do, such as, "Stand on one leg" or "Poke your tongue out". Write each thing on a piece of brightly-coloured paper.

2. Find a prize, maybe a lollipop, and wrap it in newspaper. Next add a forfeit, then another layer of newspaper and so on until you run out of forfeits. Your parcel is now ready for the game.

3. Get your friends to sit in a circle and ask a grown-up
to play the music for you. When the music starts,
pass the parcel to your left. Keep passing it round
the circle until the music stops. Whoever is
holding the parcel unwraps one layer
and has to do the forfeit for
twenty seconds. Repeat until
all the layers are gone.

The winner gets
the lollipop!

Rubbish Paper Flowers

Maggie and Rose are making a recycled flower bouquet for their grannies. They are doing a super double R – REUSING paper and REDUCING by not buying new flowers.

STUFF TO USE

Newspaper

Old magazines

String

Sticky tape

1. Fold a piece of newspaper in half lengthways.

2. Hold the paper in the middle of the fold and bunch into a flower shape.

3. Hold upside down and tie the base of the bunch together with string. This is your flower head.

4. To make the stems, take four pages from a magazine and roll into a tube. Secure it with sticky tape.

5. Attach the stem to the flower head with sticky tape. Repeat the process until you have a lovely bouquet. Use different types of paper or napkins to make it extra colourful.

Eco Flower Holder

The lovely flowers Maggie and Rose have made need something to live in. Oscar has actually made a very arty vase!

1. Cut the top off a juice carton (make sure it is washed out).

2. Turn the paper plate upside down and glue the juice carton to it.

3. Cut up old fabric into small squares.

4. Glue the squares onto the vase mosaic-style. Make sure you cover the whole thing and pay special attention to the join of the carton to the plate.

flowers by oscar

Eco Ball

Oscar and Bentley are super-keen to make an eco ball because they've invented some eco superhero games to play with it.

STUFF TO USE

Newspaper

Plastic bags

String

1. Scrunch up a few pieces of newspaper into a tight ball. Place in a plastic bag, then continue to pack more in until you have a ball as big as your head.

2. Finish layering with another plastic bag, then tie string around the ball like a net to hold it together.

Eco Ball-a-Rooney

STUFF TO USE

Masking tape

1. Using masking tape, make a target on a wall.

2. Stand fifteen paces away from the wall and kick your ball at the target. See who can hit the target the most times.

Eco Bowl-a-Rama

1. Mark out the length and width of your bowling alley with masking tape. It should be about fifteen paces long by three paces wide.

2. Weight the plastic bottles slightly with water, then screw the lids back on.

STUFF TO USE

10 plastic bottles with lids

Masking tape

3. Arrange the bottles in a triangular shape at one end of the alley.

4. Bowl your ball down the alley. For every bottle you knock down, you score one point. If you knock down all ten bottles, you score twenty points – that's called a strike!

Oscar — Strike
Maggie — 9
Rose — Strike
Bentley — 🐾

Play on your own, or with friends.

Eco Art Supplies

Rose has found some really useful recipes in Granny's secret book! (Warning — this is very, very messy!)

Make Your Own Paint

Did you know that a long, long, long time ago artists made paint from egg yolks? Maybe that's why there are so many pictures of soldiers!

1. Get a grown-up to crack an egg and separate the yolk from the white. Put the yolk in a small bowl. Save the white for later.

2. Beat in a few drops of food colouring with a fork.

3. Make enough different colours to paint a picture.

Paint a picture. When it's dry, brush the egg whites from step 1 over it. This helps protect your painting and stops it fading.

Make Your Own Brushes

If you want to paint a picture, you'll need a brush!

1. Roll six sheets of newspaper into a tight tube.

2. Wrap sticky tape around one end and wind it almost all the way down to the other end.

STUFF TO USE

Newspaper

Sticky tape

Scissors

3. Cut the unstickytaped end into bristles for your brush. This should be done with a grown-up. You can make different sizes of brush by using more or less paper.

Now paint!

Make Your Own Glue

Making glue to stick stuff with is seriously easy.

STUFF TO USE

Flour

Bowl and spoon

Water

1. Put some flour and water in a bowl and mix. The mixture should be smooth and runny, not thick and lumpy! Add food colouring, glitter or flower petals to make it pretty.

Eco Moulding Clay

This is a very easy and fun way to make Clay, which you can then make lots of fun stuff with.

STUFF TO USE

1 cup flour

½ cup sawdust

Bowl and wooden spoon

1 cup water

1. Stir the sawdust and flour together in a bowl.

2. Add a small amount of water and mix. Carry on adding water and mixing until you have a lump that feels like clay. If the mix becomes too wet, add more flour. If it becomes too crumbly, add more water and a small amount of flour.

Now you've got a lovely lump of clay to make crazy stuff with.

What are you going to make?

Eco Moulding Clay Inspiration Page

Maggie has made a sculpture of Bentley.

1. Mould your clay into a Bentley shape. Make sure it is as smooth as possible, with no visible cracks.
2. Paint on a base colour and leave to dry.
3. Paint in the detail.
4. Leave to dry, then seal with egg white or varnish.

Rose has made a necklace.

1. Shape your clay into lots of little beads.
2. Poke a hole through the middle of each bead with a straw.
3. Leave to dry for 24–48 hours.
4. Paint them.
5. When the paint is dry, thread them onto a piece of string.

Oscar has made a wormy bowl.

1. Roll out lots of worm shapes as long and thick as you like.
2. Make a round clay base for the worms to sit on.
3. Take a worm and wind it round the edge of the base. Add more worms on top. Go as high as you like. Make sure your worms are firmly stuck together.
4. Paint and leave to dry.

Eco Sculptures

Even some grown-up artists use rubbish to create their masterpieces. One artist made a polar bear out of plastic bags! See what you can make with all the rubbish in your house.

STUFF TO USE

As much clean rubbish as you can find

Sticky tape

Glue

Paint

1. First find as much interesting rubbish as you can and lay it out.

2. Think about what you may like to make. How big is it going to be?

The most fun is in the making of your sculpture, so just go for it. Play some fun music and let your imagination go wild!

Rubbish Town

Create your own play town using rubbish!

1. First make some roads by tearing off strips of newspaper and laying them on the floor.

2. Use your boxes to make buildings. First paint them all different colours and let them dry.

3. Decide which box will be which building. You could have different shops, a bank, a school, a police station – whatever you like! Make a sign for each building.

4. Cut out squares of tin foil to make windows for your buildings. Stick them on with glue. Draw the doors on with felt-tip pens.

5. Make trees to line your roads by stuffing newspaper in the tops of toilet roll tubes. Then paint your trees green.

STUFF TO USE

Newspaper

Boxes

Paint

Tin foil

Glue

Felt-tip pens

Toilet roll tubes

Wow! Your very own eco town!

STUFF TO USE

Newspaper

Glue

Tin foil

Sticky tape

Kitchen roll tube

Rockin' Recyclers

Oscar loves to sing, so he is putting together his own rockin' recycling band!
He will be the singer, Rose is on drums and Maggie and Bentley are on the shakers.
This song will be LOUD.

Microphone

1. Scrunch a sheet of newspaper into a ball, then wrap the ball in tin foil. This will be the top of your microphone.

2. Fix the top of the microphone to the kitchen roll tube with sticky tape.

3. Glue strips of newspaper to the base.

Sing away! LOUD!

Drums

STUFF TO USE

Plastic containers

Old magazines

Sticky tape

1. Lay out a selection of empty plastic containers.

2. Roll up some magazine pages into a tight tube and wind sticky tape all the way down. Do this twice to make two drumsticks.

Shakers

STUFF TO USE

Plastic containers with lids

Rice

Sticky tape

1. Half-fill your plastic containers with rice.

2. Put the lids on and seal them with sticky tape.

Now Sing! Shake! Bang!

Eco Pirates

In olden days, pirates sailed all round the world to find treasure. Sadly, Oscar and Bentley don't have a ship, so they are going to make their own eco treasure instead. That's pretty close to being a pirate from olden days!

Treasure Chest

Making your own treasure chest is much easier than finding one, because pirates always hide their treasure well.

STUFF TO USE

Sticky tape

Shoe box

Newspaper

Glue

Paint

1. Sticky tape the lid onto one side of your shoebox so it can open.

2. Keeping the lid open, paper-mâché the whole thing and leave it to dry.

3. Paint the treasure chest and leave it to dry.

Now you can fill it with loot!

Silver Coins

Pirates love silver coins. When they find them they get excited and shout things like "pieces of eight!".

1. Find any old lids and bottle tops you can. Jam jar lids are good for giant coins, whilst milk carton lids are good for mini coins.

2. Cover the lids with tin foil. Make sure you squash the tin foil tightly round the coins.

STUFF TO USE
Lids and bottle tops

Tin foil

Paper Jewels

Pirates like to wear jewellery because a pirate with lots of jewels is obviously a good pirate.

1. Find lots of interesting, colourful pages in your magazines and cut them into strips.

2. Make the strips into a paper chain using sticky tape.

STUFF TO USE
Old magazines

Sticky tape

Scissors

Make all different sizes for bracelets and necklaces.

Stuff Sorter

Maggie and Rose have invented a stuff sorter to keep all their stuff in, using all the little plastic containers they could find.

STUFF TO USE

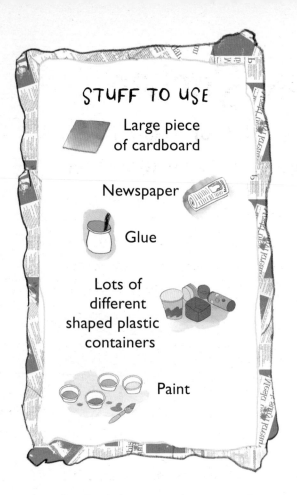

Large piece of cardboard

Newspaper

Glue

Lots of different shaped plastic containers

Paint

1. Collect some interesting shaped boxes and containers.

2. Lay your cardboard flat and arrange your containers on it.

3. Glue each container down.

4. Paper-mâché the whole thing (see Super Paper-Mâché page) and leave to dry.

5. Now paint!

Sort your stuff!

Hanging Pen Sorter

Oscar has been collecting a lot of toilet rolls and has found a really useful way to use them.

STUFF TO USE

- Toilet rolls
- Sticky tape
- Glue
- Old magazines
- Scissors
- Tin foil
- Strip of card

1. Place toilet rolls in a line and fasten them together with sticky tape.

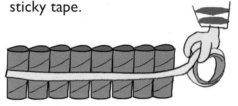

2. Stick your strip of card to the bottom of your line of toilet rolls with lots of little bits of sticky tape.

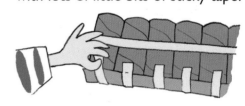

3. Lay the toilet rolls on some tin foil and cover the entire length, tucking it into the tops of the rolls (remember to leave them open at the top). Repeat until fully covered.

4. Cut letters out of an old magazine to spell out P-E-N S-O-R-T-E-R then glue them on.

Now sort your pens!

Superhero Eco Game

Maggie and Rose have made an eco superhero game
to see who is the greenest of them all.
Being green doesn't mean you might be a frog.
It means you are particularly good
at helping to save the earth.

STUFF TO USE

Paper

Pencil

Cup

Newspaper

Make your own dice

1. Write the numbers 1–6 on individual bits of paper.

2. Fold them up tightly and put them in a cup.

Make your game board

1. Get twenty sheets of newspaper big enough for you to stand on.

2. Lay them out on the floor like a trail of stepping stones, in whatever shape you like.

How to Play the Game

1. Decide which square is the start and which is the finish.

2. Find a prize for the finishing point and leave it on the square.

3. Use yourselves as counters.

4. To decide who goes first, get everyone to pick a number out of the dice cup. The one with the highest number starts.

5. Hold the cup above your head and pick a number. Move forward that number of squares, then pass the dice to the next player.

Now play!

It's a race to the prize — who will win?

Did You Know?

We use over six billion glass bottles and jars each year. It would take you over three and a half thousand years to sing "Six Billion Green Bottles"!

Every person creates the same weight in rubbish each year as five whole cars.

What other amazing eco facts can you find out? Use your computer to look some up.

This is the universal sign for recycling.

Every year we fill so many bins with rubbish that if we stacked them on top of one another, they would reach all the way to the moon.